CHERNOBYL EXPLOSION

HOW A DEADLY NUCLEAR ACCIDENT FRIGHTENED THE WORLD

by Michael Burgan

Content Adviser: Michael Wert, PhD
Associate Professor of History
Marquette University

COMPASS POINT BOOKS
a capstone imprint

Compass Point Books are published by Capstone,
1710 Roe Crest Drive, North Mankato, Minnesota 56003
www.mycapstone.com

Editor: Catherine Neitge
Designer: Catherine Neitge
Media Researcher: Svetlana Zhurkin
Library Consultant: Kathleen Baxter
Production Specialist: Laura Manthe

Scientific Adviser: Frank Summers, PhD, Outreach Astrophysicist,
Space Telescope Science Institute

Image Credits
Alamy: Leslie Garland Picture Library, 5; AP Photo: Igor Kostin, 17, Rolf Petersson,
6; Dreamstime: Yitao Liu, 29, 56 (bottom); DVIC: NARA, 22, 56 (top); Getty Images:
AFP/STF, 7, AFP/Stringer, 32, Sygma/Igor Kostin, 35, 39, 43, TASS, 25, TASS/
Valentin Kunov, 24, TASS/Vladimir Samokhotsky, 26; Granger, NYC: ITAR-TASS Photo
Agency, 10; Newscom: AFLO, 49, akg-images, 15, 47, iPhoto Inc./Menno Meijer,
50, Reuters/STR/Vladimir Repik, 46, 54, Reuters/Stringer/Vladimir Repik, cover,
41, 59, SIPA/Shone Necic V., 33, 44, 57, SIPA/Ukrinform/Zufarov/Repik, 13; Photo
from the Collection of National Museum "Chernobyl" (Kyiv, Ukraine), 37, 58 (top);
Shutterstock: Everett Historical, 19, 21, Harvepino, 8 (inset), Maryna Shkvyria, 53,
OBJM, 58 (bottom), Peteri, 8 (map), Roberts Vicups, 55, SSvyat, 31

Library of Congress Cataloging-in-Publication Data

Names: Burgan, Michael, author.
Title: Chernobyl explosion : how a deadly nuclear accident frightened the world / by
Michael Burgan.
Description: North Mankato, Minnesota : Capstone Press, [2018] | Series: CPB grades
4-8. Captured science history | Includes bibliographical references and index. |
Audience: Age 10-14.
Identifiers: LCCN 2017037861 (print) | LCCN 2017041957 (ebook) | ISBN
9780756557522 (eBook PDF) | ISBN 9780756557447 (hardcover) | ISBN
9780756557485 (paperback) Subjects: LCSH: Chernobyl Nuclear Accident, Chernobyl,
Ukraine, 1986—Juvenile literature. | Environmental disasters—Juvenile literature. |
Nuclear power plants—Accidents—Ukraine—Chernobyl—Juvenile literature.
Classification: LCC TK1362.U38 (ebook) | LCC TK1362.U38 B87 2018 (print) | DDC
363.17/99094777—dc23
LC record available at https://lccn.loc.gov/2017037861

TABLEOFCONTENTS

ChapterOne
UNSEEN MENACE

The workday was just starting on Monday, April 28, 1986, for Bengt Bellman, a safety inspector at the Forsmark nuclear power plant in Sweden. He quickly became concerned when alarms went off in the plant. The flashing lights meant sensors had detected higher than normal levels of radiation.

The plant, like others around the world, generated electricity by tapping the immense amounts of energy stored in the nucleus of radioactive materials. The radioactive materials release energy that boils water. Steam from the boiling water turns turbines that generate electricity. Nuclear power plants do not pollute the air, as coal-powered plants do. And after the cost of building a plant, it is fairly cheap to produce electricity from nuclear power. But as Bellman and other workers in his industry knew, nuclear power has a downside. Unseen radiation is deadly in large doses. That's why engineers who design and build nuclear power plants work hard to make sure radiation cannot leak out into the buildings or the surrounding areas.

Bellman and other safety officials worked quickly to find the source of the excess radiation so they could decide what to do. What Bellman learned surprised him. The Forsmark plant's workers had

Early detection of radiation by inspectors at the Forsmark nuclear plant in Sweden helped alert the world.

high levels of radiation on the bottoms of their shoes. But they had not passed through any parts of the plant where there might have been a radiation leak. Investigating further, plant officials found abnormal amounts of radiation outside the plant. Then they got reports of high levels of radiation outside another Swedish nuclear power plant. Government officials in Stockholm began to suspect that the radiation was coming from outside Sweden, but no country had reported a nuclear accident.

A Swedish inspector checked the ground for radiation the day after it was first noted at Forsmark.

The sleuthing went on, in an effort to pinpoint the source of the radiation. Devices set up across Sweden showed that radiation levels had begun to increase the day before. The rising levels were in the southeastern part of the country. A look at the weather for the previous few days showed that winds had come from that direction. It seemed possible that the winds had carried the radiation over the Baltic

A Swedish farmer wore protective clothing as he worked in an area contaminated by radiation.

Sea, from the direction of the Soviet Union. But when Swedish officials asked the Soviet government about a possible radiation leak, the Soviets denied that there had been one.

During the day Monday, news of the activity at Forsmark spread throughout Sweden. Some people wondered whether they should stay inside. Government officials measured the radiation on

BELARUS

RUSSIA

POLAND

☢ Chernobyl

⭐ Kiev

UKRAINE

Dnieper

SLOVAKIA

HUNGARY

MOLDOVA

ROMANIA

Radiation was detected in Sweden (green on globe inset), nearly 1,000 miles (1,600 km) from Ukraine.

vehicles and inspected buildings that could shelter people if a massive leak occurred. Finally, that evening, the Soviet government admitted that its country was the source of the radiation. It issued a brief statement: "An accident has occurred at the Chernobyl nuclear power plant as one of the reactors was damaged. Measures are being taken to eliminate the consequences of the accident. Aid is being given to those affected. A government commission has been set up."

But those words didn't tell the world what only a small number of Soviet officials had known for several days. Something terrible had happened at

What had started as a planned shutdown for one of the plant's four reactors had turned into a radioactive nightmare.

Chernobyl, leading to the release of large amounts of radiation into the air. But no one knew then the full extent of the accident's harmful effects.

The Chernobyl facility was in the town of Pripyat, in Ukraine, which borders central Europe. At the time, Ukraine was one of the 15 republics in the Soviet Union. The largest and most powerful republic was Russia. The Soviet capital of Moscow was there. Officials in Moscow had not quickly reported the accident at Chernobyl for several reasons. The government did not want to panic people who lived near the plant. And the officials wanted to keep the accident as secret as possible. The Soviets had a history of covering up mistakes and accidents. They wanted the world, and their own citizens, to think the Soviet Union did not make mistakes. They wanted to prove that their form of government, communism, was better than the system used in the United States and other democratic countries.

Along with those concerns, Soviet leaders were still struggling to get accurate information about what had happened at Chernobyl. They knew the first reports of disasters were sometimes wrong, incomplete, or contradictory. But although the leaders didn't know it yet, this was the situation at Chernobyl: What had started as a planned shutdown for one of the plant's four reactors had turned into a radioactive nightmare. The accident and the

government's response to it would also play a role in
the fall of the Soviet Union several years later.

In a nuclear power plant, the reactors are the
sources of the power used to generate electricity.
At the heart of each reactor is the reactor core. In
Chernobyl each core was about 39 feet (12 meters)
wide and 22 feet (6.7 m) tall. Inside the reactor
core were rods of the radioactive metal uranium,
surrounded by graphite, the material used to make
pencil lead. The graphite helped to control the process

that released energy from the uranium atoms. Rods made of boron alloys also helped control the speed of the nuclear reaction.

Reactors at nuclear power plants are regularly shut down for maintenance. On April 25, workers at Chernobyl's reactor number 4 prepared to begin the shutdown process. This shutdown, however, was different from most. Chernobyl officials had agreed to run a test on the reactor. The heat produced in the reactor by the uranium boiled water to produce steam, which turned large turbines that created electricity. The officials wanted to find out whether the turbines could spin long enough to keep producing electricity until backup power sources came on.

Having electricity at a nuclear power plant is crucial for operating it safely. The electricity powers pumps that keep cool water flowing through the reactors. Without this cooling, the reactors would overheat, causing a meltdown. The uranium fuel rods would melt and collect at the bottom of the reactors. The radioactive mass could even cut through the steel meant to contain radioactive material. Huge amounts of radiation would then be released into the air outside.

The test on reactor number 4 also included shutting down emergency safety systems designed to keep the nuclear reaction under control. When officials at other reactors were asked to conduct a similar test, they refused, thinking it was too dangerous. But the chief engineer at Chernobyl, Nikolai Fomin, agreed to do the test. He and some of the other plant engineers had no background in nuclear physics and did not have the proper training to run the test. They did not fully realize the dangerous situation that the test could create.

Shortly after midnight on April 26, after a delay the day before, the test began. The reactor's power fell rapidly—too rapidly. With several key safety controls deliberately turned off as part of the test, the engineers running the plant had to act quickly. They had two options. One was to stop the experiment. The other was to immediately get the reactor running again.

The deputy chief engineer in charge that night, Anatoly Dyatlov, chose to increase the speed of the nuclear reaction. He ordered another engineer, Leonid Toptunov, to do so. At first Toptunov refused. An angry Dyatlov said he would find someone else to do it. Toptunov, who was only 26 and hadn't been at the job long, decided not to anger his boss further. He increased the reaction speed by removing some of the boron control rods in the reactor. Now the reactor had too few control rods in it to be safe. Still, the test went on. At 1:22 a.m. on April 26, Dyatlov told the men in the control room, "Another two or three minutes, and it will all be over! Get moving, boys!"

Less than a minute later, the engineers shut off the turbine that created electricity for the plant and

"Another two or three minutes, and it will all be over! Get moving, boys!"

RADIATION ALL AROUND

The amount of radiation still lingering at Chernobyl was checked five months after the accident.

Earth and everything on it contain, and are surrounded by, various forms of energy. Light and radio waves are energy. They are also forms of radiation. The term refers to energy emitted as waves or particles. Many common items such as rocks and plants emit small amounts of radiation. The human body does too. In low doses radiation is not harmful, and it can be useful. X-rays and some treatments for cancer rely on radiation. Radioactive materials can also be used to determine the age of ancient objects.

In large doses, however, radiation can cause sickness or death. Scientists have worked out formulas that show how much radiation people can be exposed to over a certain length of time before their risk of health problems increases. Protective gear, such as gas masks and special clothing, can also reduce exposure to radiation. During a nuclear power plant accident, radioactive substances called radioisotopes release radiation. The isotopes decay—they release energy and matter from their atoms' nuclei at definite rates, which are measured by half-lives. A half-life is the amount of time it takes a radioactive substance to release half of its radioactive energy.

The iodine-131 released at Chernobyl, for example, has a half-life of about eight days. After eight days, half of it will have decayed. In another eight days, half of that amount will decay, and then the process repeats until the iodine isotope is gone. But some radioisotopes, such as the cesium-137 released at Chernobyl, have half-lives measured in years. That means areas exposed to these isotopes remain radioactive for decades.

beyond. The water meant to cool the reactor began to heat quickly. The nuclear reaction speed began to rise even more, with the absence of the cooling water and too few control rods in the reactor. Toptunov realized the situation was getting dangerous. He pressed a button to return the 205 withdrawn control rods into the reactor. But in this case, instead of slowing the reaction, the graphite tips on the ends of the rods increased it. The tips themselves did not control the reaction. Only the upper parts of the rods, about 3 feet (91 centimeters) above the graphite ends, did that. As the tips entered the water, they increased the rate of reactivity, and the power in the reactor surged. The power surge, in part, was because of a design flaw in the reactor itself. But the decisions the engineers had made earlier that night added to the disaster that followed.

The control rods got stuck and stopped moving before the upper parts, which could control the reaction, entered the water. With the power surge, steam and hydrogen gas in the reactor exploded. Another explosion quickly followed. In the control room and other parts of the building, the blasts shook concrete walls, some of them 3 feet (91 cm) thick. In the reactor building, the explosion tossed the reactor's 1,000-ton (907-metric ton) radiation shield into the air. Outside reactor number 4, people watched as flames shot out of a hole in the reactor's roof that had been created by an explosion. Pieces of burning material from the reactor

Radioactive smoke and steam billowed from reactor number 4 after a series of explosions.

also flew into the air. Some of the burning material was graphite and some was highly radioactive nuclear fuel. It fell on the roofs of surrounding buildings. The steam and smoke that billowed from the reactor building was also radioactive. They created a cloud that rose thousands of feet into the air, and the wind began to carry the cloud to the surrounding areas.

In the seconds after the first explosion, deputy chief engineer Dyatlov worried about a meltdown. He ordered workers to open valves to flood the reactor with water. He sent others to try to lower the control rods. But the blast had ruined the control rods and the rest of reactor number 4. When someone told Dyatlov that the reactor was destroyed, he refused to believe it. He went to check on the reactor himself. Seeing that the burning debris from the explosion had started several fires, he called out the plant's fire department. Then, at the reactor building, he saw a burning red glow where the reactor had been.

Throughout the night, firefighters struggled to put out the rooftop fires, while plant workers suffered with injuries caused by fire and falling chunks of concrete. Radiation levels were extremely high and unsafe.

Word of the disaster quickly spread to Chernobyl officials who hadn't been at work. They didn't know that the reactor had exploded, and at first they thought the situation was under control at the plant. Slowly, though, the officials in Ukraine and Moscow realized the reality of the crisis. The reactor had been destroyed, and large amounts of radioactivity were still being released.

Almost two weeks after April 26, the government let three of its own photographers document the damage. The photos showed the gaping hole in the

roof above reactor number 4 and the blackened remains of part of the building. The pictures gave the world its first glimpse of some of the effects of the worst nuclear power plant accident in history.

ChapterTwo
THE PATH TO CHERNOBYL

The world first saw the dangerous potential of nuclear energy at the end of World War II when the United States dropped two bombs on Japan. During the war, the United States and several of its allies had raced to build a weapon that used the atomic power of radioactive materials. President Franklin Roosevelt and some of his advisers had feared that one of their two major enemies at the time, Germany, was working on the same kind of weapon. Before the war started, in 1939, two German scientists had discovered a process called nuclear fission. They had bombarded the nucleus of uranium atoms with tiny atomic particles called neutrons. This process had split the atoms, releasing more neutrons and energy.

As other scientists learned of the discovery of nuclear fission, they saw that it could be used to produce bombs with tremendous destructive power. The key was creating a chain reaction. The neutrons produced when one atom of uranium is split can then split other atoms of the uranium, and the process keeps repeating, releasing more energy each time. The key to using nuclear power effectively was to control the chain reaction. In tests, U.S. scientists used graphite and control rods to start and manage the first chain reaction.

A U.S. plane dropped an atomic bomb on Hiroshima, Japan, on August 6, 1945, killing thousands.

A British report at the time suggested that just 25 pounds (11 kilograms) of uranium could create the same explosive force as 1,800 tons (1,633 metric tons) of the explosive TNT. Along with that destructive power, the report said such a bomb's radiation "would make places near to where the bomb exploded dangerous to human life for a long period." Yet the scientists also realized that by controlling the fission process, nuclear energy could have productive, peaceful purposes. Small reactors could power ships for months at a time. Larger ones could generate electricity for entire communities.

During the war, scientists working for the Allies developed the first atomic bombs. The United States, however, tried to keep the work secret from one of its main partners in the war against Germany—the Soviet Union. Although it and the United States were fighting a common enemy, neither government completely trusted the other. Under its communist system, the Soviet Union had tried to create a classless society in which all property was owned by the state in the name of the people. Many Americans feared that the Soviets wanted to destroy capitalism. The capitalistic economic system practiced in the U.S. and many other countries promotes the private ownership and use of property for individual profit. Capitalist nations are mostly democratic. Ideally, their people choose their leaders in fair elections.

The Soviets, however, allowed only one political party—the Communist Party—and severely limited their citizens' freedoms. People could not start their own businesses, and the government controlled most property. The United States feared the Soviet government's desire to spread its restrictive system around the world. And the U.S. leaders directing the effort to build the atomic bomb did not want the Soviets to learn about it. The Soviets, though, had spies in the Manhattan Project, the name of the U.S. program to build the bomb.

In July 1945, the U.S. government tested the first atomic bomb in the desert of New Mexico. By then,

A mushroom cloud emerged after an atomic bomb was detonated on July 16, 1945, in New Mexico.

A shrine gate was one of the few structures to remain standing after a bomb was dropped in August 1945 on Nagasaki, Japan.

Germany had been defeated, but the United States was still at war with Japan. To end the war, President Harry Truman decided to drop two of the new bombs on Japan. The first bomb and its immediate aftermath killed more than 80,000 people in the city of Hiroshima. Nuclear radiation killed many survivors, even years later. About 140,000 deaths have been blamed on the bomb. After the United States dropped a second nuclear bomb, on Nagasaki, Japan surrendered.

"Now we have our atomic sword and can start thinking about peaceful uses for the atom."

But with the war over, a different kind of conflict was about to begin. When the fighting ended in Europe, the Soviet Union controlled large parts of Eastern Europe. It quickly set up communist governments in several countries, which were under Soviet control. The United States knew the Soviets would try to continue to spread their influence around the world. The two countries began what was called the Cold War. Their armies rarely engaged in direct conflict. But each government sent money and weapons to various countries and rebel groups, trying to earn their loyalty. That aid was designed to help weaken the other's power around the globe.

In the context of the Cold War, the Soviet Union scrambled to build its own nuclear weapons. Thanks in part to what it learned from its spies in the Manhattan Project, the Soviets were able to build a bomb, which was tested in 1949. Scientist Igor Kurchatov had led the Soviet effort to build the bomb. After the successful test, he said, "Now we have our atomic sword and can start thinking about peaceful uses for the atom."

Within five years of its first bomb test, the Soviet Union had built a nuclear reactor that could generate electricity. It was the first one in the world to produce power for commercial use. The water in the reactor boiled to produce steam, but soon both Soviet and American scientists were trying to create

Workers at a Soviet nuclear power plant watched as a basket filled with nuclear fuel was lifted in 1964.

pressurized water reactors. In that type of reactor, water was heated, but pressure kept it from boiling. The hot water then moved to a separate compartment, where its heat made more water boil, creating steam to power the turbines. This system allowed less radioactive water to reach the turbines. But Soviet scientists and engineers struggled to perfect the pressurized water reactor. The Soviets then focused on building larger boiling-water reactors, which were called RBMKs. These reactors could be refueled

Some Soviet scientists were worried about the safety of nuclear power plants in the 1960s and 1970s.

while they were operating, and the Soviets thought they were safe, so they didn't feel the need to build expensive containment structures around them.

During the early 1970s the Soviet Union began building its first nuclear power plants that used RBMK reactors. The building proceeded even though some scientists pointed out flaws in the system. One flaw was the possibility of a power surge under certain conditions. The British government considered the design so unsafe that it would never let any of its power plants use a similar reactor. Some Soviet scientists also had concerns about the reactor's safety. In public, though, engineers such as Nikolai Fomin insisted that Soviet reactors had plenty of safety features to prevent accidents.

The plan for the power plant to be built near Pripyat, Ukraine, called for six reactors, each able to produce 1,000 megawatts of electricity—roughly enough to provide power to 700,000 homes per year. The site was close to the border with the Soviet republic of Belarus and about 80 miles (129 km) from the Ukrainian capital of Kiev, which would receive

Construction of the Chernobyl plant began in 1970. Work on reactor number 4 was completed in 1983.

most of the plant's electricity. Pripyat was a new town, built just for the power plant and the workers who would run it. The plant's official name was the V. I. Lenin Nuclear Power Station. Vladimir Lenin had been the first leader of the Soviet Union. But the plant was more commonly called Chernobyl, for the name of a small town nearby.

Soviet leaders took pride in their technological achievements, such as putting the first person into space in 1961 and undertaking huge construction projects. The Soviet Union had once been a fairly poor nation focused on agriculture. Under the communist system, it had industrialized quickly, though many people still lived as poor farmers in the area around Pripyat and across the country. In Soviet thinking, Chernobyl and other massive power plants like it were a sign of communism's superiority. That was one reason Soviet officials never disclosed problems that had occurred at other nuclear plants with RBMK reactors.

Several accidents had taken place during the mid-1970s at a plant west of the city of Leningrad (present-day St. Petersburg). An accident in 1974 killed three people and released a small amount of radiation. The next year, a reactor core at the plant partly melted, releasing large amounts of radiation. Soviet officials even hid the details of these and other accidents from people who worked at other nuclear plants. As novelist and historian Piers Paul Read wrote, the Soviet workers had "little opportunity to learn from the mistakes of others."

The first Chernobyl reactor began producing power in 1977, and the second one started operating the next year. While two of the other four planned reactors were under construction, in March 1979 the world's attention turned to an accident at the Three Mile Island nuclear plant near Harrisburg, Pennsylvania. Soviet officials blamed that accident on capitalism. They argued that the company that ran the plant was more interested in making money than in taking safety precautions. Soviet leaders continued to stress that their country's reactors were safe.

They continued to make that case in public even after an accident at Chernobyl's first reactor in 1982. A problem with the cooling system led to the melting of some uranium, which created a small explosion. Radiation leaked into the reactor building, and some also escaped and drifted over Pripyat. Some workers were exposed to high levels of radiation, but no one told the people of Pripyat what had happened. Meanwhile, work continued on reactor number 4, which opened the next year.

When the events of April 26, 1986, began to unfold, the people of Pripyat did not have to be told about the accident at the Chernobyl plant. They could see it with their own eyes.

ACCIDENT IN PENNSYLVANIA

Cooling towers sent steam into the sky at the Three Mile Island nuclear plant.

On the morning of March 28, 1979, a mechanical or electrical failure shut down water pumps at unit 2 of the Three Mile Island nuclear power plant. The reactor shut down, but another systems failure led workers to think an open valve was actually closed, as it was supposed to be. Radioactive cooling water from the reactor core poured through the valve, leading to a partial meltdown.

U.S. government officials and the news media learned about the accident near Harrisburg, Pennsylvania, within hours, unlike their counterparts in the Soviet Union after the Chernobyl disaster. Radioactive gases escaped the plant, and for several days some officials worried that a bubble of hydrogen inside the reactor container would explode, releasing more radiation. That didn't happen, but thousands of people left the area near the plant.

Government officials later determined that the average amount of radiation released during the accident was about the same amount a patient would receive during a chest X-ray. Still, the reactor never reopened, and the accident sparked a debate in the United States about the safety of nuclear power. Fueling the discussion was the movie *The China Syndrome*, which had been released just 12 days before the accident. The fictional story described the possible dangers of a major nuclear meltdown.

After the Three Mile Island accident, the number of new U.S. nuclear power plants built dropped dramatically. Still, as of 2017 the country had almost 100 reactors, which produced about 20 percent of its electricity.

ChapterThree
SLOWLY REVEALING THE TRUTH

Early in the morning of April 26, the day of the disaster, Vasily Ignatenko was in a fire station at the Chernobyl plant when he and the other firefighters heard the explosions from reactor number 4. From their station they could see flames shooting out of the reactor building. So could Ignatenko's wife, Lyudmilla. The two were newlyweds, and they lived in the fire station with several other couples. As Vasily went to his truck, he told his wife to go back to sleep. "I'll be back soon," he said.

Ignatenko and the other firefighters didn't know what had caused the explosions and the fire. But they were trained to do a job, so they went up onto the roofs of the buildings to battle the blazes. The heat turned the roofing material into a sticky mess, like fresh tar. In their rush to fight the fire, the men didn't wear their usual canvas clothing—not that it would have protected them from the radiation pouring out of the damaged reactor.

Inside the plant, workers tried to find missing coworkers and open valves to release water into the reactor. Readings from the radiation-detecting dosimeters told them they were being exposed to high levels of radiation. The signs of radiation sickness came quickly—headaches, difficulty breathing,

A monument in the town of Chernobyl honors the firefighters who died in the nuclear plant disaster.

nausea, swollen skin. Some of those exposed saw their skin turn brown—a nuclear tan, the people of Pripyat soon called it. Outside the plant, guards were limiting who could enter the facility. Some handed out potassium iodide tablets, which were designed to limit the harmful effects of iodine-131 on the body.

Coverage of the Chernobyl disaster was slow to appear on Soviet TV.

As the disaster unfolded on the morning of April 26, plant officials continued to downplay the problem. Plant director Viktor Bryukhanov told a Communist Party official in Moscow that everything was under control. In the Soviet Union, the Communist Party was the true source of government power. Keeping a good job or getting a better one meant joining the party and not questioning its leadership. Men like Bryukhanov worked hard to keep their party bosses happy. Bryukhanov believed the reports he received that no radiation

Mikhail Gorbachev did not make a televised statement about the disaster for more than two weeks after the accident.

had been released. Perhaps he also wanted to believe it, because he did not want to have to report that a serious accident had occurred. And like other important officials at the plant, he was not an expert in nuclear power.

Although Bryukhanov didn't know the true nature of the disaster, some Soviet military officials had a better grasp of the situation. At 3:30 a.m. a general ordered units trained to handle nuclear accidents to go to the plant. As the morning went on, the general called Soviet leader Mikhail Gorbachev, telling him the situation might be worse than had first been reported. Gorbachev and his advisers, however, were slow to react to the crisis. They did not plan to meet to discuss it for two days.

As the sun rose that Saturday morning, Vasily Ignatenko, like the other firefighters, knew how dangerous the radiation leak was. By 7 a.m. he was in the hospital, suffering from radiation sickness. Guards kept his wife, Lyudmilla, from entering the building, but a friend who was a doctor there helped Lyudmilla get in. "He's bad," the doctor told her. "They all are." Lyudmilla soon saw for herself. Her husband's face was so swollen that she could barely see his eyes. He was dead within two weeks. Some nurses and doctors who treated Ignatenko and the other firefighters later got sick too. They had absorbed radiation coming off their patients' bodies.

With no word about the nature of the accident, the people of Pripyat went about their lives on a warm and sunny spring day. Soviet students attended school on Saturdays, and Alexandr Sirota went to class as usual. He was thinking about the new amusement park in town that was scheduled to open on May 1, May Day, a major holiday in the Soviet Union. His teacher left the room to attend an emergency meeting, and he and the other students heard rumors about an accident at the power plant. They saw military helicopters and emergency vehicles gathered at the hospital across the street. Alexandr left the school and went to a nearby bridge, hoping to see what was happening at the plant. Other people joined Alexandr on the bridge, trying to glimpse the activity around reactor number 4. Earlier, before sunrise, adults had flocked to the bridge, admiring the glowing debris that had filled the sky as if it were a fireworks show. They didn't know they were being exposed to large doses of radiation. Later the residents of Pripyat called the spot where they had stood watching "the bridge of death."

Through the day on Saturday, more government officials learned the true nature of the problem—the reactor had exploded, and radiation was still being released. Blocks of graphite were still on fire, and radioactive water was coming out of the plant. On Sunday morning, local officials in Pripyat made an

Later the residents of Pripyat called the spot where they had stood watching "the bridge of death."

Once buses arrived in Pripyat, the evacuation went very quickly.

announcement over loudspeakers: "In the interest of the safety of the people, which is a priority to us, there is reason to evacuate." The announcement told people to take only a few basic items, since the evacuation would only last a few days. As he prepared to ride on one of the 1,100 buses sent to Pripyat, Alexandr packed a small suitcase. He considered the evacuation a short adventure. But he and his neighbors would never return to their homes again.

Residents of nearby villages also were told to evacuate. The government set up an exclusion zone within a 19-mile (30 km) radius of the Chernobyl plant. Some older farmers failed to understand the dangers of radiation, since they could not see it, and they still felt well. A man told them they had to leave their animals behind: "The cows, sheep and goats are radioactive, especially their coats." People had to go without their dogs and cats as well.

By then, Soviet officials had decided to try to use sand to put out the fire still burning at reactor number 4. Huge helicopters began dumping tons of sand on the reactor building. Later they dropped chemicals to extinguish the fire. But the copters' spinning blades stirred up radioactive dust outside the plant. The crew members flying the helicopters received large doses of radiation when they opened the doors to release the sand. On the ground, many of the officials now working in Pripyat were feeling symptoms of radiation sickness, but not so badly that they went to the hospital. They stopped eating food from local farms, in case it was contaminated.

Mikhail Gorbachev met with his advisers on April 28 to discuss the situation in Chernobyl. They decided to make their first public statement about the accident. But they argued over how many details they should release. Meanwhile, relying on faulty sources, a news service reported that 2,000 people were

THE FIRST IMAGES

The photographers sent by the Soviet government on May 9 to view the damage to Chernobyl's reactor number 4 were not the first photographers on the scene. Less than 12 hours after the explosion, plant officials sent Anatoly Rasskazov, who worked at Chernobyl as the staff photographer, in to photograph the damage. At first he flew above the reactor, leaning out of a helicopter while a soldier held his legs. Then he approached it on the ground in a fire truck.

While working, Rasskazov was exposed to radiation. He later said, "By 11:00 in the evening, I could hardly walk. My skin had turned red and I couldn't stop vomiting." Soviet officials seized all his work. Only two of his photos were ever published. One appeared on Soviet TV in May 1986, but it did not show the full scale of the disaster. Officials retouched the second photo, removing, Rasskazov said, "the ray of light emanating like a burning sun from the reactor, along with the smoke, ash and other flakes of material." Rasskazov blamed radiation at Chernobyl for the cancer and blood diseases that he battled after his exposure. He died in 2010 at the age of 66.

Anatoly Rasskazov, staff photographer at the Chernobyl nuclear power plant, took a photo of reactor number 4 only hours after the explosion.

dead after the explosion. A report in *The New York Times* noted that Ukrainian officials had criticized the "inferior quality of construction and installation work" at Chernobyl and another plant.

While still keeping the details secret, the Soviet government finally announced that two plant workers had died during the accident, and some towns had been evacuated. The Soviets asked for help from West Germany and Sweden in fighting the fire. Meanwhile, around Pripyat, soldiers and volunteers arrived to help remove the radioactive debris. That included scraping up contaminated soil from the ground. Some wore thin medical masks, not the more effective devices that could screen out radiation in the air they breathed.

The troops and volunteers were called liquidators, because they tried to liquidate—eliminate—all the dangerous material. They arrived to find a ghost town. As one liquidator later said, "The village street, the field, the highway—all of it without any people." Some of the men were ordered to shoot the dogs and cats roaming the empty streets, since they were contaminated too.

On May 9 three government photographers were allowed to go to the plant and photograph the damage and cleanup effort. One was Volodymyr Repik. Wearing protective clothing and a cloth mask, he flew in a helicopter above the scene. In one photo, he

"The village street, the field, the highway—all of it without any people."

shot a helicopter dropping chemicals on the reactor. Another showed a man with a dosimeter measuring radiation around the plant.

As Repik worked from the air, Igor Kostin joined a group of liquidators working on a roof near the

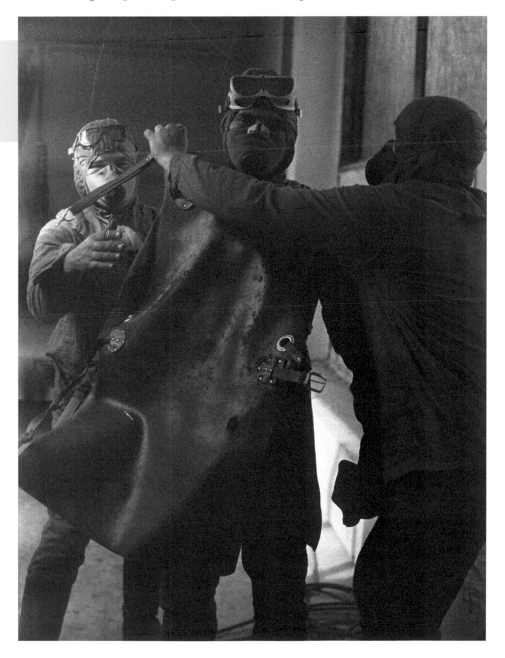

Igor Kostin photographed liquidators donning protective gear they made from lead sheets.

reactor. As they shoveled radioactive debris, Kostin clicked away on his camera. The soldiers near him counted to 20. It was too dangerous for the photographer to remain on the highly radioactive roof for more than that time.

When they were done, Repik, Kostin, and a third photographer, Valery Zufarov, gave their film to the government. All cameras at the time used film that needed to be developed before the pictures could be seen, and Soviet officials wanted to tightly control the images it would release to the public. The Communist Party newspaper, *Pravda*, finally published its first photo of the Chernobyl disaster on May 12. It was one of Repik's, and it showed the huge hole in the reactor building, its sides blackened by the fire. The picture, which had been released by the state-owned news agency TASS, was reprinted in newspapers around the world.

TASS also issued a statement saying that six people had died. "In the past 24 hours," it said, "work was considerably broadened at the Chernobyl nuclear power station to clean up the contaminated sections of the territory and structures of the station." Yet people outside the Soviet government still didn't know exactly what had happened or about the danger that Chernobyl still posed.

Volodymyr Repik's aerial view of the destruction to reactor number 4 appeared in newspapers worldwide.

ChapterFour
LIFE AND DEATH IN UKRAINE

On May 1, 1986, May Day festivities went on as planned in Moscow and Kiev. The Moscow parade featured long lines of the country's weapons, and Mikhail Gorbachev attended, as major Communist Party leaders always did. He still had not said anything in public about the Chernobyl disaster, which he knew still posed a threat to Soviet citizens. He had not visited the site or met with victims of radiation poisoning. In Kiev, local party officials attended their city's holiday celebration. But it was rumored that many had sent their families outside the city, fearing that radiation could drift over Kiev. By then, several countries in Europe had reported increased levels of radiation in the atmosphere.

Government leaders in Moscow continued to debate how much information they should disclose. *Pravda* finally ran a story on May 6 with more details of the accident. The highlights of the article were released by TASS and reported around the world. The story praised the bravery of the firefighters who first went to the scene and said the situation was "under control." The newspaper article also criticized news agencies outside the Soviet Union for spreading false reports of the number of people killed or exaggerating the dangers of the radiation released.

A May Day celebration went on as planned in Kiev, despite the potential for severe radiation problems.

The *Pravda* story asked, "What can be more shameful than to gloat over the trouble that occurred?"

But the report seemed to downplay the accident. Radiation levels around Kiev sometimes rose, depending on how the wind blew. And some people were not quickly treated for radiation sickness. Shortly after the accident, Soviet nuclear engineer Grigori Medvedev wrote, "The truth of the matter is that no one was prepared for the Chernobyl phenomenon."

Gorbachev made his first public statement about Chernobyl on May 14. He stressed that the government would investigate what happened and make sure it would not happen again. He said seven people had died from radiation exposure and several hundred were being treated for radiation sickness.

After the accident, the Soviets set up check points in the danger zone around Chernobyl to check for radiation.

Most of the radioactive materials emitted had a half-life of 30 years, but one radioisotope had a half-life of 2 million years.

He also admitted, "Extensive and long work still lies ahead. The level of radiation in the station's zone and on the territory in the immediate vicinity still remains dangerous for human health." Gorbachev thanked foreign scientists and nations that had offered aid. But as the *Pravda* story had done, he attacked some nations—especially the United States—for carrying out an "anti-Soviet campaign." Even in this time of crisis, Soviet leaders believed, Cold War activities were continuing.

Soon after the speech, Soviet officials announced they would begin building a concrete structure around the damaged reactor, to try to contain some of the radiation. The structure was called a sarcophagus, which means a stone coffin. Soviet experts said the sarcophagus, which was built to last 30 years, would have to stay in place for centuries to contain the radiation from the nuclear fuel still in the reactor. Most of the radioactive materials emitted had a half-life of 30 years, but one radioisotope had a half-life of 2 million years.

Liquidators began building the sarcophagus while others continued the cleanup around the Chernobyl plant. More than 600,000 liquidators in all helped with the effort. Some workers believed the false rumor that drinking vodka would protect them from the radiation all around them. The Soviet government brought in robotic vehicles to remove contaminated

Workers who built the sarcophagus posed in November 1986 with a banner that read "We shall fulfill the government's goal."

debris, but not all of them worked well. So people did most of the work, receiving much higher doses of radiation than was safe. They did not die quickly, as had some Chernobyl workers and firefighters who had been there when the accident happened. Some liquidators died years later, of cancer and other diseases associated with radiation.

Viktor Bryukhanov (left) and Nikolai Fomin, along with Anatoly Dyatlov, were sentenced to 10 years in a labor camp after a three-week trial in July 1987. Three other officials received shorter labor camp sentences.

The sarcophagus was finished by the fall of 1986. Some of the people evacuated were allowed to return home, but not the people of Pripyat. It remained empty, with houses left just as they had been in April.

Gorbachev and others thought that his new policy of *glasnost*—openness—had worked during the disaster. Though it took some time, many details about the accident were released, unlike the Soviet government's handling of previous nuclear accidents. The government put on trial several of the men who had directed the plant and the test the night of April 26. They were accused of failing to follow safety regulations at "explosive-prone enterprises." Nikolai Fomin, Anatoly Dyatlov, and Viktor Bryukhanov were among those who went to prison.

But with the Chernobyl accident, many average Soviet citizens lost trust in their government. They had believed the promises about the safety of nuclear power. Now the people saw that these things were not true. Reports spread about the poor quality of the building at Chernobyl and the inexperienced people who ran some of its operations. And with the policy of glasnost still in place, more Soviet citizens voiced their complaints about living in a country that restricted freedoms and had huge amounts of poverty. Indeed, the accident made Gorbachev seek more openness within his government, since he saw how information was distorted or held back.

At the time of the accident, he later said, even he was astounded that it had happened. "Nuclear scientists," he said, "had always assured the country's leadership that our nuclear reactors were completely safe."

Gorbachev worked to slow the arms race with the United States. He also tried to carry out reforms in the Soviet Union. He introduced a policy called *perestroika*—Russian for "restructuring." He slowly weakened some of the government's control over the economy. He also gave local governments more freedom to act as they chose, instead of always following orders from Moscow. But his efforts were not enough to preserve the Soviet Union. At the end of 1991, the country split into 15 nations. Years later, Gorbachev said the Chernobyl meltdown, "even more than my launch of perestroika, was perhaps the real cause of the collapse of the Soviet Union."

After gaining their independence, Ukraine and Belarus had to deal with the effects of Chernobyl on their own. The final death toll for the number of people killed in the first few weeks after the April 1986 meltdown was 30, all but two from radiation. But medical experts knew that some effects of radiation sickness would take years to develop. Government officials checked on the health of many of the liquidators to see whether they got sick. Some of the workers exposed to the highest radiation doses seemed to have a higher risk of developing leukemia, a form of cancer.

Years later, Gorbachev said the Chernobyl meltdown, "even more than my launch of perestroika, was perhaps the real cause of the collapse of the Soviet Union."

MELTDOWN IN JAPAN

A nuclear accident in Japan in 2011 drew new attention to the accident that had happened in Chernobyl 25 years earlier. On March 11, a tsunami created by an earthquake sent a wall of water into the Fukushima Daiichi Nuclear Power Station. The tidal wave caused a partial meltdown in three of the plant's reactors, releasing radiation into the air and contaminating food and water supplies. Since then, radioactive water from the plant has entered the Pacific Ocean.

No deaths have been linked to the radiation released since the accident or during the cleanup

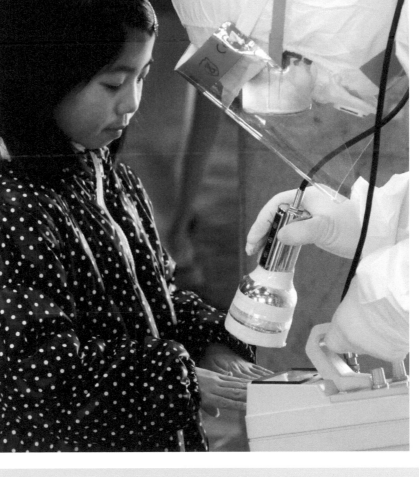

A young girl was checked for radiation a few days after the Fukushima meltdown. She lived about 20 miles (32 km) from the nuclear plant.

efforts. But some Japanese fear the long-term effects of radiation that was released during the accident. Some people have called on the electric company that owned the plant to seal it with a sarcophagus, as was done in Chernobyl. Plant officials insist, however, that they can safely remove the radioactive material still there. In 2017 the company was pumping 400 tons (363 metric tons) of water through the damaged reactors every day. The contaminated water was then stored in large tanks. The protective gear workers wear is also collected and stored. Each of the 6,000 workers cleaning the plant gets a new protective suit every day. The process of cleaning up the Fukushima site could cost almost $200 billion and take decades.

Chernobyl also affected mental health. Many people who lived in the area had developed "radiophobia." They worried that illnesses they had developed were caused by radiation, when in almost all cases there was no relationship. Decades later, some people still showed increased anxiety about their health and often described physical symptoms that doctors could not link to a disease.

Children who drank contaminated milk after the accident were also affected. By 2016 about 11,000 children had developed thyroid cancer, and a few

A nurse stood outside a room of children who were treated for thyroid cancer in Minsk, Belarus, in 1998. The cancer cases were linked to the Chernobyl accident years earlier.

cases were most likely connected to exposure to iodine-131 in the milk. Some parents in the region affected by the radiation also reported having deformed babies. They blamed their exposure on Chernobyl radiation, which a 2010 study bore out. Parents who were children in 1986 and then had their own children as adults saw other health problems in their kids, including stomach and lung troubles. In recent years, some Ukrainian children have eaten locally grown mushrooms and berries with levels of radiation that are considered unsafe.

A Belarus doctor named Nadezhda Burakova recalled what her daughter thought about how radiation could affect her future children. The girl told Burakova, "If I give birth to a damaged child, I'm still going to love him." That girl and the mother had fled their home right after the accident. Burakova said her own sister had not wanted to take them in at the time, fearing they would spread radiation. Years later, Burakova said, many people still disliked being around "Chernobyl refugees."

With each milestone anniversary of the events of April 26, 1986, some journalists have looked back at the Chernobyl explosion and what followed. Reporters visiting the area in 2016 found that Pripyat was still largely a ghost town, though tourists could explore parts of the exclusion zone for short periods. A few hundred people, most of them elderly, had gone back to live in their homes in the zone. In Ukraine, officials warned shortly after the accident that the vegetables they grew were probably contaminated. But the "self-settlers" were not concerned. The government sends doctors to check on them—just one part of an effort to monitor the health of more than 2 million Ukrainians after the Chernobyl disaster. Almost one quarter of them are children. Russia has a similar health program for about 900,000 people.

Belarus, which was badly affected by the radiation, does not share information on the aftermath of Chernobyl. Like the Soviet Union before the days of glasnost and perestroika, Belarus is a dictatorship that tightly controls all government information. Yury Bandazhevsky was a scientist who studied the damaging effects of radiation in Belarus. He spoke out against the way the government had handled health problems related to Chernobyl. He was arrested and jailed in 1999, then left Belarus after his release. He said in 2016, "For me, the problem of Chernobyl is not finished, it has only just begun. I am very much afraid that in one or two generations from now, the [descendants] of the population of Belarus and Ukraine that were affected by Chernobyl will vanish."

Without much human activity in the exclusion zone, wildlife have returned to the region—despite the high levels of radiation in some areas. Scientists

Wild horses run free in the Chernobyl exclusion zone, which is filled with wildlife.

have warned that the radiation affects some animals. Voles, relatives of mice, have more eye problems, and the population of some birds has fallen. And while some animals have adapted and are doing well in Belarus and Ukraine, reindeer in Norway are still eating food contaminated by radiation that drifted from Chernobyl. The food made the reindeer radioactive too. Some reindeer raised for meat still can't be eaten.

By 2016 international health experts said that as many as 9,000 people will eventually die from cancers linked to Chernobyl radiation. Other scientists said the death toll could be much higher. Of the three photographers who traveled to the damaged nuclear plant in May 1986, two died of diseases

Volodymyr Repik, who photographed the destruction of Chernobyl, died of a radiation-related illness in 2012.

caused by radiation. Igor Kostin died in a 2015 car accident, but he also suffered from diseases linked to radiation. Volodymyr Repik, who took the photo of Chernobyl seen around the world, had these thoughts before he died: "If I had been ordered now to get aboard [a helicopter] and go, I would not have gone—you might have easily died there for nothing."

Today a new sarcophagus surrounds the remains of Chernobyl's reactor number 4. The concrete of the original one had begun to crumble, and so several dozen nations helped Ukraine build a new one.

The arch-shaped containment structure over the nuclear plant today looms next to the abandoned town of Pripyat.

The new containment structure is 800 feet (244 m) wide and 350 feet (107 m) high. It was rolled into place over the reactor in 2016 and is designed to last at least 100 years. Ukrainian officials hope to use remote-controlled devices during that time to remove the radioactive material still inside the reactor.

While that work goes on, the empty town of Pripyat and the people affected by radiation-related diseases remind the world what happened at Chernobyl during the early hours of April 26, 1986. The accident also made it clear that while nuclear power has peaceful purposes, accidents can unleash its destructive force. As a result, nuclear plants have added steps to increase safety, and scientists remain watchful.

Timeline

1945

The United States drops atomic bombs on Hiroshima and Nagasaki, Japan, in August, leading to the end of World War II

1977

The first of four reactors at the Chernobyl nuclear power plant begins producing electricity

1979

A reactor at the Three Mile Island nuclear power plant has a partial meltdown

1954

The Soviet Union creates electricity with the world's first commercial nuclear reactor

1974

An accident at a nuclear power plant near Leningrad kills three people and releases radiation into the air

1985

Mikhail Gorbachev becomes the leader of the Soviet Union

Timeline

April 26, 1986

An accident at Chernobyl destroys one of the plant's reactors and releases large amounts of radiation

April 28, 1986

The Soviet Union admits there has been an accident at Chernobyl

March 11, 2011

An earthquake and tsunami trigger a triple meltdown at Japan's Fukushima Daiichi nuclear power plant

May 9, 1986

Volodymyr Repik photographs the damage at Chernobyl, and three days later one of his pictures is released

1991

The Soviet Union breaks up into 15 countries

2016

Experts estimate that as many as 9,000 people and perhaps many more will die from radiation from the Chernobyl accident; Ukraine places a new containment structure over the damaged reactor

Glossary

allies—people, groups, or countries that work together for a common cause; when capitalized, refers to the United States and its allies during major wars

arms race—the effort between two or more nations to build the biggest and best weapons

atom—smallest unit of a chemical element; atoms contain electrons, protons, and neutrons

communism—system in which goods and property are owned by the government and shared in common; communist rulers limit personal freedoms to achieve their goals

containment—the act or process of keeping something from spreading

contaminated—made unfit for use by a harmful substance

dosimeter—device used to measure radiation

evacuate—leave an area to escape a natural or human-made disaster

exclusion zone—area into which entry is forbidden

industrialized—dependent on businesses instead of farming as the main source of income

nuclei—plural of nucleus, the dense core of an atom that contains protons and neutrons

radioactive—having to do with materials that give off potentially harmful invisible rays or particles

retouch—in photography, to make changes to a picture after it was taken, often to change or remove something from the original image

Additional Resources

Further Reading

Johnson, Rebecca L. *Chernobyl's Wild Kingdom: Life in the Dead Zone*. Minneapolis: Twenty-First Century Books, 2015.

Marquardt, Meg. *The Science of a Nuclear Plant Explosion*. Ann Arbor, Mich.: Cherry Lake Publishing, 2016.

Owen, Ruth. *Energy from Atoms: Nuclear Power*. New York: PowerKids Press, 2013.

Rissman, Rebecca. *Swept Away: The Story of the 2011 Japanese Tsunam*i. North Mankato, Minn.: Capstone Press, 2017.

Internet Sites

Use FactHound to find Internet sites related to this book.
Visit *www.facthound.com*
Just type in 9780756557447 and go.

Critical Thinking Questions

What role did the Cold War play in the Soviet Union's refusal to disclose nuclear accidents in a timely fashion? Did things change much when Mikhail Gorbachev came to power? Use examples from the text when framing your answer.

Why do some people consider nuclear power a better way to generate electricity than burning coal? What do you think about nuclear power? Does it have a bright future?

How was the response to the Chernobyl accident different from what happened after the 1979 accident at Three Mile Island?

Source Notes

Page 8, line 5: Serge Schmemann. "Soviet Announces Nuclear Accident at Electric Plant." *The New York Times*. 29 April 1986. 28 Sept. 2017. http://www.nytimes.com/1986/04/29/world/soviet-announces-nuclear-accident-at-electric-plant.html

Page 12, line 25: Grigori Medvedev. *The Truth About Chernobyl*. Trans. Evelyn Rossiter. New York: Basic Books, 1991, p. 69.

Page 20, line 1: "Report by MAUD Committee on the Use of Uranium for a Bomb." 1943. Nuclear Files.org. 28 Sept. 2017. http://www.nuclearfiles.org/menu/key-issues/nuclear-weapons/history/pre-cold-war/manhattan-project/maud-report.htm

Page 23, line 20: Piers Paul Read. *Ablaze: The Story of the Heroes and Victims of Chernobyl*. New York: Random House, 1993, p. 7.

Page 28, line 2: Ibid., p. 41.

Page 30, line 10: Svetlana Alexievich. *Voices from Chernobyl: The Oral History of a Nuclear Disaster*. Trans. Keith Gessen. New York: Picador, 2006, p. 5.

Page 33, line 22: Ibid., p. 6.

Page 35, line 1: Kim Hjelmgaard. "Chernobyl Disaster 30 Years Later." *USA Today*. 2016. 29 Sept. 2017. https://www.usatoday.com/pages/interactives/chernobyl

Page 36, line 7: *The Truth About Chernobyl*, p. 189.

Page 37, col. 1, line 18: "Iranian Journalists in America; Chernobyl Anniversary." CNN. 28 April 2006. 29 Sept. 2017. http://edition.cnn.com/TRANSCRIPTS/0604/28/i_c.01.html

Page 37, col. 1, line 24: "Chernobyl Voices: Anatoly Rasskazov." BBC News. 14 Dec. 2006. 29 Sept. 2017. http://news.bbc.co.uk/2/hi/europe/6177927.stm

Page 38, line 3: "Soviet Announces Nuclear Accident at Electric Plant."

Page 38, line 19: *Voices from Chernobyl: The Oral History of a Nuclear Disaster*, p. 35.

Page 40, line 20: "TASS Statement on Chernobyl Accident." Associated Press. 12 May 1986. 29 Sept. 2017. http://www.apnewsarchive.com/1986/Tass-Statement-on-Chernobyl-Accident/id-996c529015a1c3c930f03f0f6c2414ce

Page 43, line 1: Associated Press. "Soviet Statement and TASS Dispatch on Chernobyl Accident." *The New York Times*. 6 May 1986. 29 Sept. 2017. http://www.nytimes.com/1986/05/06/world/soviet-statement-and-tass-dispatch-on-chernobyl-accident.html

Page 44, line 4: *The Truth About Chernobyl*, p. 207.

Page 45, line 1: Associated Press. "Excerpts from Gorbachev's Speech on Chernobyl Accident." *The New York Times*. 15 May 1986. 29 Sept. 2017. http://www.nytimes.com/1986/05/15/world/excerpts-from-gorbachev-s-speech-on-chernobyl-accident.html

Page 47, line 13: *Ablaze: The Story of the Heroes and Victims of Chernobyl*, p. 228.

Page 48, line 2: "Gorbachev Weighs Chernobyl Legacy." BBC News. 24 April 2006. 29 Sept. 2017. http://news.bbc.co.uk/2/hi/europe/4918940.stm

Page 48, line 15: "Chernobyl 30 years later: A nuclear disaster that brought down an empire." *The Economist*. 26 April 2016. 29 Sept. 2017. http://www.economist.com/news/europe/21697741-chernobyl-led-thousands-deaths-including-soviet-union-nuclear-disaster

Page 51, line 15: *Voices from Chernobyl: The Oral History of a Nuclear Disaster*, p. 193.

Page 51, line 21: Ibid., p. 194.

Page 52, line 20: "Chernobyl Disaster 30 Years Later."

Page 54, line 5: Anna Melnichuk. Photographers recall Chernobyl's first days." NBC News. 24 April 2011. 29 Sept. 2017. http://www.nbcnews.com/id/42738018/ns/world_news-europe/#.Wc6W2kzMxcA

Select Bibliography

"1986–2016: Chernobyl at 30." World Health Organization. 25 April 2016. 29 Sept. 2017. http://www.who.int/entity/ionizing_radiation/chernobyl/Chernobyl-update.pdf?ua=1

Alexievich, Svetlana. *Voices from Chernobyl: The Oral History of a Nuclear Disaster.* Trans. Keith Gessen. New York: Picador, 2006.

Associated Press. "Excerpts from Gorbachev's Speech on Chernobyl Accident." *The New York Times.* 15 May 1986. 29 Sept. 2017. http://www.nytimes.com/1986/05/15/world/excerpts-from-gorbachev-s-speech-on-chernobyl-accident.html

Associated Press. "Igor Kostin, photographer who captured the Chernobyl disaster, dies at 78." *The Guardian.* 10 June 2015. 29 Sept. 2017. https://www.theguardian.com/world/2015/jun/10/igor-kostin-photographer-chernobyl-disaster-dies-78

Associated Press. "Looking back: 30 years of photographing Chernobyl." *Daily Mail.* 21 April 2016. 29 Sept. 2017. http://www.dailymail.co.uk/wires/ap/article-3552014/Looking-30-years-photographing-Chernobyl.html

Associated Press. "Soviet Statement and TASS Dispatch on Chernobyl Accident." *The New York Times.* 6 May 1986. 29 Sept. 2017. http://www.nytimes.com/1986/05/06/world/soviet-statement-and-tass-dispatch-on-chernobyl-accident.html

"Backgrounder on Chernobyl Nuclear Power Plant Accident." United States Nuclear Regulatory Commission. 12 Dec. 2014. 29 Sept. 2017. https://www.nrc.gov/reading-rm/doc-collections/fact-sheets/chernobyl-bg.html

"Chernobyl Accident 1986." World Nuclear Organization. November 2016. 29 Sept. 2017. http://www.world-nuclear.org/information-library/safety-and-security/safety-of-plants/chernobyl-accident.aspx

"Chernobyl 30 years later: A nuclear disaster that brought down an empire." *The Economist.* 26 April 2016. 29 Sept. 2017. http://www.economist.com/news/europe/21697741-chernobyl-led-thousands-deaths-including-soviet-union-nuclear-disaster

"Chernobyl Voices: Anatoly Rasskazov." BBC News. 14 Dec. 2006. 29 Sept. 2017. http://news.bbc.co.uk/2/hi/europe/6177927.stm

Daniloff, Nicholas. "Chernobyl and Its Political Fallout: A Reassessment." *Demokratizatsiya*, Vol. 12, No. 1. January 2004. pp. 117-132.

DeYoung, Karen. "Swedes' Nuclear Sleuthing." *The Washington Post.* 4 May 1986. 29 Sept. 2017. https://www.washingtonpost.com/archive/politics/1986/05/04/swedes-nuclear-sleuthing/6de34959-59ca-4e5a-a681-9587545e4311/?utm_term=.5809bcf0fb2c

Fountain, Henry. "Chernobyl: Capping a Catastrophe." *The New York Times.* 27 April 2014. 29 Sept. 2017. https://www.nytimes.com/interactive/2014/04/27/science/chernobyl-capping-a-catastrophe.html?hp&_r=0

Gillette, Robert. "Chernobyl Design Flaws Made Accident Worse, Soviet Report Concedes." *Los Angeles Times.* 23 Aug. 1986. 29 Sept. 2017. http://articles.latimes.com/1986-08-23/news/mn-15781_1_design-flaws

"Gorbachev Weighs Chernobyl Legacy." BBC News. 24 April 2006. 29 Sept. 2017. http://news.bbc.co.uk/2/hi/europe/4918940.stm

Higginbotham, Adam. "Half-life: 25 Years after the Chernobyl meltdown, a scientific debate rages on." *Wired UK.* 5 May 2011. 29 Sept. 2017. http://www.wired.co.uk/article/half-life

Hjelmgaard, Kim. "Chernobyl Disaster 30 Years Later." *USA Today.* 2016. 29 Sept. 2017. https://www.usatoday.com/pages/interactives/chernobyl

Karmanau, Yuras. "AP Exclusive: Ukraine Children Eat Food Tainted by Chernobyl." Associated Press. 22 April 2016. 29 Sept 2017. https://apnews.com/6571b70ca68441caadc7d069bc27e7ad/ap-exclusive-ukraine-children-eat-food-tainted-chernobyl

Manning, Elizabeth. "The events of Chernobyl." UPI. 17 April 1996. 29 Sept. 2017. http://www.upi.com/Archives/1996/04/17/The-events-of-Chernobyl/4546829713600/

Medvedev, Grigori. *The Truth About Chernobyl.* Trans. Evelyn Rossiter. New York: Basic Books, 1991.

Nechepurenko, Ivan, and Henry Fountain. "Giant Arch, a Feat of Engineering, Now Covers Chernobyl Site in Ukraine." *The New York Times.* 29 Nov. 2016. 29 Sept. 2017. https://www.nytimes.com/2016/11/29/world/europe/chernobyl-disaster-cover.html

"Nuclear Power in the USA." World Nuclear Organization. September 2017. 29 Sept. 2017. http://www.world-nuclear.org/information-library/country-profiles/countries-t-z/usa-nuclear-power.aspx

"Nuclear Reaction: Why Do Americans Fear Nuclear Power?" *Frontline.* PBS. 22 April 1997. 29 Sept. 2017. http://www.pbs.org/wgbh/pages/frontline/shows/reaction/etc/script.html

"Photographers Recall Chernobyl's First Days." Photos. NBC News. 24 April 2011. 29 Sept. 2017. http://photoblog.nbcnews.com/_news/2011/04/24/6521313-photographers-recall-chernobyls-first-days

Potter, William C. "Soviet Decision-Making for Chernobyl: An Analysis of System Performance and Policy Change." National Council for Soviet and East European Research. March 1990. 29 Sept. 2017. https://www.ucis.pitt.edu/nceeer/1990-802-12-Potter.pdf

"RBMK Reactors." World Nuclear Association. June 2016. 29 Sept. 2017. http://www.world-nuclear.org/information-library/nuclear-fuel-cycle/nuclear-power-reactors/appendices/rbmk-reactors.aspx

Read, Piers Paul. *Ablaze: The Story of the Heroes and Victims of Chernobyl.* New York: Random House, 1993.

"Report by MAUD Committee on the Use of Uranium for a Bomb." 1943. Nuclear Files.org. 28 Sept. 2017. http://www.nuclearfiles.org/menu/key-issues/nuclear-weapons/history/pre-cold-war/manhattan-project/maud-report.htm

Rich, Motoko. "Struggling With Japan's Nuclear Waste, Six Years After Disaster." *The New York Times.* 11 March 2017. 29 Sept. 2017. https://www.nytimes.com/2017/03/11/world/asia/struggling-with-japans-nuclear-waste-six-years-after-disaster.html?_r=0

Robinson, Melia. "Reindeer Are Still Very Radioactive 30 Year After Chernobyl." *ScienceAlert.* 23 Dec. 2016. 29 Sept. 2017. https://www.sciencealert.com/reindeer-are-still-very-radioactive-30-years-after-chernobyl

Rubin, David M. "How the News Media Reported on Three Mile Island and Chernobyl." *Journal of Communication*, Vol. 37, No. 3. September 1987, pp. 42–57.

Schmemann, Serge. "Soviet Announces Nuclear Accident at Electric Plant." *The New York Times.* 29 April 1986. 28 Sept. 2017. http://www.nytimes.com/1986/04/29/world/soviet-announces-nuclear-accident-at-electric-plant.html

Schofield, Matthew. "Ruined Chernobyl nuclear plant will remain a threat for 3,000 years." McClatchy DC Bureau. 24 April 2016. 29 Sept. 2017. http://www.mcclatchydc.com/news/nation-world/world/article73405857.html

Semenov, B.A. "Nuclear power in the Soviet Union." *IAEA Bulletin*, Vol. 25, No. 2. June 1983. International Atomic Energy Agency. https://www.iaea.org/sites/default/files/25204744759.pdf

Stern, Mark Joseph. "Did Chernobyl Cause the Soviet Union to Explode?" *Slate.* 25 Jan. 2013. 29 Sept. 2017. http://www.slate.com/articles/health_and_science/nuclear_power/2013/01/chernobyl_and_the_fall_of_the_soviet_union_gorbachev_s_glasnost_allowed.html

"TASS Statement on Chernobyl Accident." Associated Press. 12 May 1986. 29 Sept. 2017. http://www.apnewsarchive.com/1986/Tass-Statement-on-Chernobyl-Accident/id-996c529015a1c3c930f03f0f6c2414ce

Wendle, John. "Animals Rule Chernobyl Three Decades After Nuclear Disaster." *National Geographic.* 18 April 2016. 29 Sept. 2017. http://news.nationalgeographic.com/2016/04/060418-chernobyl-wildlife-thirty-year-anniversary-science/

Index

About the Author

Michael Burgan has written many books for children and young adults during his 20 years as a freelance writer. Most of his books have focused on history. Burgan has won several awards for his writing. He lives in Santa Fe, New Mexico.